Little Books of Guidance
Finding answers to life's big questi...

THE WAY OF LOVE

Rest

A little
book of
guidance

CHURCH
PUBLISHING
INCORPORATED

Unless otherwise noted, the Scripture quotations contained herein are from the New Revised Standard Version Bible, copyright © 1989 by the Division of Christian Education of the National Council of Churches of Christ in the U.S.A. Used by permission. All rights reserved.

Scripture quotations marked (NIV) are taken from the Holy Bible, New International Version®, NIV®. Copyright © 1973, 1978, 1984, 2011 by Biblica, Inc.™ Used by permission of Zondervan. All rights reserved worldwide. www.zondervan.com The "NIV" and "New International Version" are trademarks registered in the United States Patent and Trademark Office by Biblica, Inc.™

This book compiles text from the following sources:
Amy Sander Montanez, *Moment to Moment: The Transformative Power of Everyday Life* (Harrisburg, PA: Morehouse Publishing, 2013); Stephen Cottrell, *Do Nothing to Change Your Life: Discovering What Happens When You Stop* (New York: Seabury Press, 2007); Renée Miller, *Strength for the Journey: A Guide to Spiritual Practice* (Harrisburg, PA: Morehouse Publishing, 2011); "The Spirituality of Everyday Life" by Cecilia Andrews and "Entering the Emptiness" by Gerald May in *Simpler Living, Compassionate Life: A Christian Perspective,* ed. Michael Schut (Denver: Church Publishing, 1999).

Church Publishing
19 East 34th Street
New York, NY 10016
www.churchpublishing.org

Cover design by Jennifer Kopec, 2Pug Design
Typeset by Denise Hoff

A record of this book is available from the Library of Congress.

ISBN-13: 978-1-64065-180-7 (pbk.)
ISBN-13: 978-1-64065-181-4 (ebook)

Printed in the United States of America

Contents

Introduction

I pray that you, being rooted and established in love, may have power, together with all the Lord's holy people, to grasp how wide and long and high and deep is the love of Christ, and to know this love that surpasses knowledge—that you may be filled to the measure of all the fullness of God.

—Ephesians 3:17–19, NIV

At the 79th General Convention of the Episcopal Church in July 2018, Presiding Bishop Michael B. Curry called the Church to practice *The Way of Love*. This is an invitation to all of us, young and old alike, to "grow more deeply with Jesus Christ at the center of our lives, so we can bear witness to his way of love in and for the world."

With this call, Bishop Curry named seven practices that can help us grow deeper in our relationship with God, Jesus, and our neighbors as we also learn how to live into our baptismal promises more fully. In today's world of busy schedules, hurried meals, and twenty-four-hour news cycles, it is now more imperative that we make and take the time to center ourselves and follow the way of Jesus. This might mean revisioning and reshaping the pattern and rhythm of our daily life—finding a slice of time to center our thoughts on Jesus. Within these pages you will find ideas to engage in the practice of rest as you walk on *The Way of Love: Practices for a Jesus-Centered Life*.

To be a Christian is to be a seeker. We seek love: to know God's love, to love, and to be loved by others. It also means learning to love ourselves as a child of God. We seek freedom from the many forces that pull us from living as God created us to be: sin, fear, oppression, and division. God desires us to be dignified, whole, and free. We also seek abundant life. This is a life that is overflowing with joy, peace, generosity, and delight. It is a life where there is enough for all because we share with abandon. We seek a life of meaning, giving back to God and living for others and not just for ourselves. Ultimately we seek Jesus. Jesus is the way of love and that has the power to change lives and change the world.

How are we called to practice the Way of Love? Bishop Curry has named seven practices to follow. Like a "Rule of Life" practiced by Christians for almost two thousand years, these are ways that help us live intentionally in our daily life, following our deepest values. These are not add-ons to our day, but ways to recognize God working in us and through us.

Jesus teaches us to come before God with humble hearts, boldly offering our thanksgivings and concerns to God or simply listening for God's voice in our lives and in the world. Whether in thought, word, or deed, individually or corporately, when we pray we invite and dwell in God's loving presence. Jesus often removed himself from the crowds to quiet himself and commune with God. He gave us examples of how to pray, including the Lord's Prayer. "Will you continue in the prayers?" "I will with God's help."

Practices are challenging and can be difficult to sustain. Even though we might practice "solo" (e.g., prayer), each practice belongs to the community as a whole in which you inhabit as a whole—your family, church, or group of friends. Join with some trustworthy companions with whom to grow into this way of life; sharing and accountability help keep us grounded and steady in our practices.

This series of seven Little Books of Guidance is designed for you to discover how following certain practices can help you follow Jesus more fully in your daily life. You may already keep a spiritual discipline of praying at meals or before bed, regularly reading from the Bible, or engaging in acts of kindness toward others. If so, build upon what we offer here; if not, we offer a way to begin. Select one of the practices that interests you or that is especially important for you at this time. Watch for signs in your daily life pointing you toward a particular practice. Listen for a call from God telling you how to move closer. Anywhere is a good place to start. This is your invitation to commit to the practices of **Turn—Learn—Pray—Worship—Bless—Go—Rest**. There is no rush, each day is a new beginning. Follow Bishop Curry's call to grow in faith "following the loving, liberating, life-giving way of Jesus. His way has the power to change each of our lives and to change this world."

1 ▪ Loafing with God

My only understanding of Sabbath as a child came from the commandment, "Remember the Sabbath day, and keep it holy" (Exodus 20:8). I believed that meant to go to church on Sundays, the Sabbath. We did our chores on Saturday, so we didn't have much house or yard work to do on Sundays, but I had no real idea about Sabbath. I did homework if it needed doing and Mom was still cooking meals. When I was a teenager I went back to church Sunday evenings for youth group, and some Sundays I got to church at 9:00 a.m. and, other than grabbing lunch, I stayed there for basketball games, cheerleading practice, and then youth group. It was wonderful and holy busyness. It formed me, but it didn't teach me how to listen for God's movement in my life, or how to allow for the Mystery in my life, or how to discern and separate my ego from God's will. In other words, it didn't transform me.

During my training as a spiritual director, I learned about Sabbath, that practice of truly resting in God. One lecture I heard during these studies encouraged observing the Sabbath an hour a day, a day a week, a weekend a quarter, a week a year, and a month every five years. An hour a day, just to loaf with God. The idea of it astonished me. What would that look like? Would I just sit still and listen? Could I walk in the garden? Chop fresh herbs? Drink a glass of wine? Listen to music? The German Lutheran in me knows how to be effective, efficient, structured. We know how to work, we German Lutherans. In my three years of confirmation class I never heard about Martin Luther resting, only that he was busy and distraught and wrote ninety-five theses. Loaf? It seemed almost sacrilegious to rest.

I have learned the practice of Sabbath over time. Learning the art of listening for God in daily meditation and contemplative prayer was a wonderful start. As I silenced my busy mind and honestly asked to hear God's truth, wisdom, and reality, holy guidance began to change my life.

About three years into my Sabbath exploration I began to take silent retreats, sometimes only a day and sometimes a weekend. This time was filled with quiet walks, prayer, mindfulness, and time in the creative process. I would be graced with poems writing themselves and pieces of scripture coming into my consciousness. I spent time in scripture, learning the process of *lectio divina*, a way of reading scripture meditatively, not theologically or academically. I would let my body sing, dance, do yoga, or whatever it felt like it needed to do to open to the Holy. I would breathe more deeply, it seemed, and my body would find a new place of rest. I spent time in nature. Long walks on the beach or in the mountains and watching the rising or setting of the sun and moon seemed to allow my own natural rhythm to return, to evolve. Sometimes I was alone. Sometimes I was with a friend.

Over the last fifteen years, what I have come to believe about the practice of Sabbath is that it is our natural, instinctive way of being. We are designed to return to our Source. Little children do it naturally. They play and then they rest, play and rest. I wish I had been taught to listen in a more concrete way as a child. I would have cherished learning a practice of silence. Listening for God instead of talking to God would have been great learning.

Some people have asked me, "When I am resting in God, what am I listening for?" Good question. It is hard to say without knowing your life's circumstances. Let me begin by reminding you that you are resting. That is all you are doing. You don't have to listen or speak. Resting is pure unto itself. However, if you are intentionally listening for the voice of God, especially if you are wishing to discern something, remember that listening is a personal experience and it begins with emptying, getting the ego and false desires out of the way. I have heard people say they hear a voice. I've never heard a voice but I've had words put into my consciousness. For example, after praying for months (thinking about, asking for God's help, crying) about a relationship that was damaged, the words that finally "came to me," not as clear words but more as a complete and whole thought, were: "It's okay for this to be over. Let it go. There's nothing more for you to do now."

Sometimes we are listening more for our own reality, or, said another way, listening for our own intuition about something. Taking time to rest, breathe, unplug, and detach allows us to hear ourselves. Our *Selves*, the God-seed in us. What does our inner wisdom have to say about something? Perhaps the answer is waiting within us and just needs time and space to find its way to the surface. When we give ourselves the gift of Sabbath, the opportunity to descend to our most personal depths is available, and very often, the answers we are seeking are right there.

For me, Sabbath is also an opportunity to pay closer attention to my dreams. I try to remember my dreams every day and often journal about the ones that stick with me long enough for me to get them written down. When I am taking intentional Sabbath, it seems my dreams are clearer, bigger, and in a way more intrusive. It is as if the Holy is finding another way to reach me. And in Sabbath, I have time to look anew at past dreams that I have written down but not spent sufficient time processing.

2 ■ Learn to Be Still

A couple of years ago I was due to lead an assembly at a Church of England comprehensive school that I visited regularly. This is a tough gig: seven or eight hundred adolescents, crowded into a hall first thing on a Monday morning, and forced to endure a hymn, a prayer, a worthy talk and, usually, a ticking off. One rises to give the talk to be greeted by a sea of faces grimacing back, as if to say, "Go on then: impress me!"

On this occasion my anxiety levels were particularly high since I had not really prepared anything much to say. It was the beginning of Lent, and I had a vague idea about encouraging them to take something on rather than give something up, but as I walked to the school I was all too aware that I was in the fast lane of the motorway, with no petrol in the tank and I had just driven past the services!

But these moments of panic can also be moments of prayer, moments when we are more open to the wiles of God. And it was almost as I got up to speak that a crazy idea was suddenly born within me. Now, I don't really know where these ideas come from. They appear to come from without and so it's hard to even categorize them as your idea at all. It is like a gift. Suddenly one is aware of what to say and what to do, and if there was time to analyze it, or even prepare it more carefully, it wouldn't have the same power. So I stood up and found myself saying something like this:

> We live in a crazy, frantic world. Our world is full of movement and noise. Even this morning in the few hours since you woke up you have probably filled your time with the radio, the TV, the computer, the PlayStation; you've probably phoned someone and texted half a dozen others. As

5

you got dressed, washed, showered, ate your breakfast, came to school, noise and busyness have been accompanying your every move. I believe many of the world's problems are caused by our inability to sit still and to be quiet and to reflect. I believe that in this season of Lent we should try to give up being so frantic, and we should take on some moments of stillness.

Then I stopped, as if I had lost my thread (actually it felt as if the thread were being handed to me inch by inch, and even I was not aware what was at the end). And I said to them, "Hey, you don't know what on earth I'm talking about, so let me give you a demonstration. Let me show you what I mean. This is what I'm suggesting that you do, each day in Lent, for exactly one minute. It will change your life."

I then picked up a chair, placed it in the center of the stage, and slowly and carefully sat down upon it, with my feet slightly apart, and with my back straight and with my hands resting gently on my knees. And for a minute I sat still. I didn't say anything, and I didn't do anything. I wasn't even consciously praying. I was just sitting there. And I breathed deeply, and I thought about my breathing. And when I reckoned the minute was over, I stood up.

But before I could say my next bit there was a huge, spontaneous round of applause. Now, I had done lots of assemblies in that school. On many occasions I had slaved over what I would do or say to capture the imaginations of the young people. But I had never had a response like this. In fact, in the days that followed, I was stopped in the street on several occasions by parents who told me that their child had come home and told them about the priest who took assembly and just sat on the stage in silence for a minute and then suggested they might do the same thing. Because when the applause died down, that's what I said. I just suggested that sitting still, being silently attentive to things deep within ourselves and things beyond ourselves, would make a difference. You didn't need to call it prayer. You didn't need to call it anything, because it would be in these moments of sedulous stillness that God could be discovered.

Like all the best sermons, I really needed to hear that one myself. I shudder to think of people who know me reading this book. I fall a long way short of the diligent day-dreaming I am recommending here, and they know it! But I believe that people will either recover this way of living and enjoying life, or they will perish. We urgently need to stop imagining everything is so urgent. Thus we will learn to nurture our inner slob.

So here is a practical way forward:

Get a chair. Not too comfy, not too hard; a dining-room chair will do. Place it somewhere quiet and peaceful. You may even wish to place it in a window so that you can look out, or have some other pleasing things to look at around you—some flowers, a candle, a picture of something lovely. But don't worry too much about this: soon you will be closing your eyes.

Now sit on the chair. Shuffle around a bit on your bottom and you will discover that at the base of your spine there is a bone for sitting on, and if you don't slouch, and if you get yourself onto it properly, then your back will be straight and you will be sitting upright and comfortable.

Now position your legs. Don't stretch them out or cross them but sit with your feet slightly apart and then rest your hands upon your legs, just above the knee. Try to have your neck straight and look straight ahead.

Now breathe carefully and deeply.

Think about your breathing. Concentrate on it and don't think about anything else for a few moments.

Feel the air being drawn into your lungs and allow your chest to swell with the air that you are receiving. And when your lungs are full—and fill them much more deeply than you usually do—hold it for a moment, and don't yet breathe out. Enjoy the sensation of your lungs gorged on air and your body still. Be attentive to this most basic function of your body—the in and out of your breathing. And then exhale the air slowly. Almost blow it out.

Then breathe again, and as you breathe in think about all the good things that you long to take into your life; all the things that you are thankful for. Maybe even count your blessings on each of your inward breaths.

As you hold the air in your lungs, be thankful for the gift of life itself. Become aware of your dependence upon the air around you and upon the taken-for-granted motions of your body.

Breathe out again, this time expelling from yourself all thoughts of irritation, bitterness, frustration, and regret. Rid yourself of the anxious, hectoring desire to be important and to be at the center. Allow yourself to be part of the creation, dependent upon the resources that come to you as a gift from outside yourself.

Then, still conscious of your breathing, but not thinking about it so much, close your eyes and allow the deep rhythm of your breathing to still your whole being. Hold the stillness and, without particularly trying, experience a greater openness to everything that is around you. At this point you may wish to turn your hands over, so that your palms are facing upwards. The slight vulnerability of this action will increase that sense of openness and express a desire to receive.

Now you are still. You are centered. You are beginning to pray. But it doesn't much matter whether you call it prayer. It is a way of being still in the midst of busyness.

I have practiced sitting still like this for many years and sometimes I have been able to remain motionless and attentive for as long as five minutes, but it is usually less. Other, far more centered people than me can sit still for hours. But it is not the length of time that matters; rather it is a case of nurturing a certain attitude to life and developing an increased desire for silence and for attentiveness.

It can be practiced anywhere: at home in a quiet moment, or on the train, or on a park bench. But it is my fervent belief that if everyone learned to sit still like this, the world would be a much happier place.

And if this sitting still seems like too much too soon for a busy person like you, then seize the opportunities that daily life offers. When the sun is shining and there are five minutes to spare, lie down in the sun. Enjoy the feeling of the heat on your skin. If you are a commuter, then from the hours you spend on the train each day, turn a few minutes into moments of contemplation. If you go for a walk, then make sure there is also a moment to stop. And if the kids will let you, lie in bed a bit longer this Saturday!

3 ■ Prayer and Meditation

Centering Prayer

We move at a pace in life that keeps our souls as busy as our bodies; our unconscious as full as our conscious minds. We are regularly challenged to switch between ideas, images, feelings, thoughts, and emotions with the speed of a computer alternating between programs. The effect on our souls is subtle and stealthy. Over time, we find it difficult simply to be still. We find it difficult to pray or believe that we are centered in the Divine Presence during prayer. When we are able to take the time to focus ourselves on communication with God, we find our minds assailed by those same ideas, images, feelings, thoughts, and emotions that plagued us before we sat down to pray. It seems that the moment we settle ourselves in God's presence, we find that we are thinking about a meeting we need to prepare for, or a soccer practice we need to shuttle our child to, or something we have forgotten to buy at the store, or the person in the hospital that needs a visit. We may force ourselves to complete the prayer period and wonder at the end of it if we've even prayed at all. Or, we may choose to truncate or postpone our prayer because we are frustrated by the constant chatter in our minds.

Centering Prayer, a contemporary version of the ancient practice of contemplative prayer, is not only a way to pray, but a way of prayer that has the potential to make a significant impact on the pattern of our lives when we are not praying. Thomas Keating, the Cistercian monk and master of Centering Prayer, says that we are not able to determine if the practice is making a difference in our souls based on what happens during the actual time spent in the practice. Rather, we know the prayer is effective in our lives by the comments we receive from others who begin to see a difference in us. When we simply sit faithfully in God's presence and stay there, even when thoughts distract us, we will find that we are able to bring the practice into the situations of our everyday lives. Instead of becoming focused on what may seem urgent but is ultimately unimportant, we find we are able to let it go, just as we have done during the course of the prayer practice itself. In other words, what we practice in the prayer is what we begin to live outside the time of prayer.

Centering prayer is a simple, though hardly easy, practice. After settling in the presence of God, we choose a sacred word as a symbol of our intent to remain in God's presence during the prayer period. As thoughts rise in us, we gently let them go and return to the sacred word. Thomas Keating uses a potent image. He says that as thoughts float across our consciousness, they are like boats on the surface of a river. When we are focused on what is on the surface of the river rather than the river itself, we slip away from our original intention. The sacred word helps call us back to the place of stillness and faithful presence to God. It is the soft offering that affirms that we want to give our attention back to God. We continue the process of letting go of thoughts and returning to the sacred word throughout the time given to the practice—usually twenty to thirty minutes once or twice each day.

If you are contemplative and reflective, you are probably easily attracted to this form of prayer. You may find that it provides respite from the rigors of daily demands. On the other hand, if you are active and highly verbal, you might, at first, think centering prayer is unsuitable for your spiritual personality. After practicing it for some time, however, you may be surprised by the spiritual balance that you experience as a result of quieting yourself in the place of deep spiritual rest.

Praying with Beads

One of the most difficult aspects of prayer and meditation is focus. So much that occurs in the daily round of life distracts us during the time of prayer. If we were to count the number of thoughts we have in just one hour, we would be astonished at the capacity of our minds to flit like hummingbirds from thought to thought. In many ways, this is not a new phenomenon. We easily fault contemporary life and technology for what Buddhists call "monkey mind." Yet, it is more a primordial than a generational response. It is part of being human and it is a glorious part of being human. It is what makes dreaming, imagining, inventing, and creating possible. While we can quickly become discouraged during prayer with the plethora of stuff inside our minds moving us off focus, it is that very stuff that is responsible for our ongoing health and growth.

The real issue is in the timing. There are times when we want to be free of our bouncing thoughts in order to become inwardly still. There are times we want our focus to be as piercing as a laser beam. There are times we do not want any disturbance to interrupt our intention. An external aid can often help us find the peace and focus we seek. For centuries, in all religions, beads and prayer ropes have been such an aid. While the most familiar use of prayer beads is as a counter for the number of prayers said, its use extends far beyond its abacus function. Prayer beads are used to help channel the mind's energy to a single point with each bead representing a mantra or a prayer. As the user moves their fingers along the beads they are connecting mind and body in such a way that the soul is able to break free to be still in the presence of God. The fingering of the beads keeps the mind and body engaged so that the soul can enter the depths of divine love.

Episcopalians are most familiar with the Anglican Rosary that was developed in the 1980s as an aid for contemplative prayer. It is essentially a blend of the Roman Catholic Rosary and the Orthodox Prayer Rope. The Anglican rosary consists of twenty-eight beads with one Invitatory bead and four cruciform beads. The thirty-three beads are prayed three times, and a prayer is said with the cross so that the total number reaches one hundred. This is the same number used for the Orthodox Prayer Rope. Anglicans also use the Roman Catholic Rosary with slight adaptations. Islam, Buddhism, Hinduism, Sikhism, and Christianity all have some form of prayer beads. There is even an application for prayer beads for use on some mobile phones.

When we begin using beads as a prayer practice, we will need a certain amount of time to become so familiar with the practice and the prayers that they are repeated by memory rather than by conscious thought. Here, the intent is to "push the play button," so that the prayers will keep the mind occupied but not really thinking. This creates the space for the soul to descend more deeply into stillness. While we are learning the practice, we will not find ourselves descending as deeply as we will once the beads and their associated prayers have become one with our minds and the beating of our hearts. When that begins to occur, we will experience the kind of meditation that leads the soul into deep rest, into the divine embrace, into that space of holiness from which no one emerges unchanged.

If you feel a desire for contemplative prayer, but find it hard to sit still or keep thoughts at bay, you will find praying with beads a

It is meant to be the soft nudge that will help us stay tethered to what is most important in our lives—union with the Divine. If we develop the pattern and practice of turning our souls to God throughout the day, we will find that our souls stay full and our hearts remain still. The ancient spiritual pattern of praying the Offices is a way of centering the soul in the presence of God throughout the day.

We often think of saying the Offices either as an outdated and uninteresting form of prayer, or as a liturgical practice that is more communal than meditative. In truth, the Offices are infinitely flexible, and many creative variations can be used while retaining the structure that, for centuries, has kept souls close to heaven.

The word "Office" comes from the Latin word *opus* meaning work. Praying the Offices, like other spiritual practices, can sometimes seem like work we would rather not do. This prayer practice, however, has the capacity to draw us into something that makes more of our souls, more of our lives, more of the world. Like a musical opus by Mozart or Beethoven, it is a work of spiritual magnitude that can easily be missed simply because we are looking for something more exciting and trendy. Yet, if we embrace the humble and repetitive, sometimes boring, daily-ness of it, we will be astonished by the enormity of its power.

Unlike some other spiritual practices, praying the Offices is both an active and a contemplative experience. It draws upon the discursive part of our beings as well as the reflective. In it we taste the textured word of God in scripture, we pray the prayers of intercession and petition, we confess the times we've missed the mark and caused separation, we acknowledge and re-commit to the faith that is in us, we get down and dirty with the daily rigors and stresses of life as we work our way through the Psalms, and we have ample time to allow the finger of heaven to etch words on our souls in silence.

There are three strategies that will help us to receive the fullest spiritual benefit from this ancient practice. First, we need to give ourselves the freedom to adapt the Offices to what is important in our own prayer styles. This makes it a more relevant practice for modern life. For example, we can substitute other Collects or write our own, we can play a favorite piece of music for a canticle, or we can do five minutes of yoga or centering prayer as a response to one of the readings. What is most important, however, is to stay with whatever pattern we choose until it becomes second nature to us. The most grace-filled element of praying the Offices is that they become a kind of mantra for deep meditation. In other words, when we have them memorized, or practically so, we stop sitting on the edge of the pool with our feet dangling in the shallow end. Instead, we jump into the deep end and find ourselves enveloped in the full water of God's embrace. If we continually change the pattern every day, we remain at the edge of the pool.

Second, we need to make a commitment to consistency. This will keep our souls regularly poised for heaven's whisper and touch. Like any other practice in life, it is the consistency of the practice that yields the results. Over time, the commitment to consistency will lead us to a place of deep desire—desire that is more profound than the simple eagerness to try something new, or experience the good feeling of having done what we thought we should do. The deeper desire is to find the Holy One when our souls are empty and dry, to be held in the rugged embrace of heaven, to taste and chew the words of God that are sometimes bitter, sometimes sweet. Perhaps, the Offices have remained such a powerful spiritual tool, precisely because they have been prayed consistently throughout the centuries. They are still prayed daily all over the globe; God's blessing has been called down into people's hearts and onto the world day after day for hundreds of years.

Third, we need to trust that even if our hearts don't feel the value of the prayer, God is there waiting to tend our languishing hearts. We need to trust enough that we are willing to wrap our hearts around the practice so tightly that it becomes natural to us even on days when words seem useless and prayers feel empty. We need to trust that when the practice is threaded into our souls like strands of wool, they will become solid and strong. We need to trust that the buffeting of the stresses and struggles of life will not interrupt or interfere with the tightly woven relationship between us and God. When we trust this much, we are more able to detach from difficulty and re-attach to ardor.

Praying the Offices is an attractive form of prayer if you find communal and liturgical prayer nourishing. It may be more difficult for you if you are tired of praying in a formulaic manner or if you feel it is a practice that is irrelevant to contemporary life, or if you prefer to simply rest in God rather than manage lectionaries, books, and Bibles. The Office, however, is an ancient prayer practice that offers more than words can express. You must try and try again until it becomes part of your day, until the day is not complete without it.

Discursive Meditation

A disciple once asked one of the desert fathers how she could know that her prayer was making a difference. "I sit in my cell in solitude and silence, but I hear nothing. When will my prayer reach heaven?"

"Do not expect that because you sit in silence, heaven will come down. Instead, chew on the words of heaven until your tongue speaks to God as you are speaking to me. Heaven will see your effort and grant you grace." The desert father was trying to explain that meditation is more than simply sitting still and waiting. It is also about thinking and reflecting. The labor of this is not lost on heaven. When God sees the seriousness we bring to the task and hears us trying to converse, God will respond.

The word discursive comes from the word discourse and refers to having a conversation. When we think of meditation, conversation is not usually what we think about. We move quickly to being silent and still, waiting on God to communicate with us in some way. It seems that prayer is composed of conversation, while meditation is composed of contemplation. In fact, meditation can include both conversation and contemplation.

Discursive meditation involves digging, speaking, and listening. When we engage in discursive meditation, we gnaw on a scriptural principle or spiritual truth like a dog with a meaty bone. We look at it from different angles, consider how it might be practiced in different situations, attempt to penetrate its nuances in order to develop new patterns of behavior that will bring us closer into the embrace of heaven. To begin, choose a scripture passage or story for the time of meditation and offer a short prayer of intention. Read the passage and reflect on it in a logical and systematic way by asking questions such as these: Who is involved here? What is actually happening? What has created the circumstances in this passage? Why do people respond as they do? What other responses are possible? How do I experience God? When do I miss the presence of God or turn from it? Where do I fit in? How can I respond to this in my own life?

The deep interior and honest reflection that we give these questions helps us grow in understanding of spiritual principles and mature in faith. When the meditation period has ended, we carry our intentions with us into daily life where prayer is actually lived.

Three elements of discursive meditation are particularly helpful in creating these new contours in our souls. First, discursive meditation engages the mind, which teasingly becomes over-active the moment we try to settle into contemplative prayer. Second, it takes us into the holy stories in a way that makes them and us real. Finally, it leads to a makeover of our souls and a behavior change in our bodies. We are no longer so willing to stand on the outside watching to see how we will be re-shaped by people and situations in our lives. Instead, we become the active participants in the drama of life, praying that we will grow more and more into the likeness of God in all circumstances and with all people in our lives.

Lest we think that discursive meditation is too heady, too logical, too left-brained, we will find that all forms of discursive meditation offer some aspect of contemplation. We use the mind to sift and sort, study and sense, but at any point in the prayer when we feel a particular affective longing rising in us for the Divine One, we simply drop down into stillness and contemplation. There, in the moments of sublime silence, we find our souls filling up and filling out, and we are gladdened with the spiritual power we experience when we simply take the time to come apart and rest awhile.

Two familiar forms of discursive meditation are *lectio divina* and Ignatian Prayer. **Lectio divina**, the pattern established by St. Benedict in the fourth century, combines elements of both discursive and contemplative prayer. The four movements of *lectio divina* include: reading, meditation, prayer, and contemplation. We begin by taking a passage of scripture and reading it slowly and deliberately—as if savoring a plate of the finest and most exquisite food. This opens the door to deep reflection and meditation. This is the point at which questions are asked, possibilities are turned over in the mind, new patterns of insight are sought, and applications of the biblical story are applied to our personal human stories.

As we enter into the passage and see the intersection between ourselves and God, we easily move into a time of discourse or conversation with God. Our spirits are moved by what we have thought and considered, what we have tasted and twirled in our mouths like fine wine, and the result is a yearning to be in an encounter of prayer with the One who is at once beyond us and as close to us as the steady beating of our hearts. When all our words have been expended, and our thoughts have been emptied into the heart of heaven, we are ready to simply rest in God. We are ready to be still. We are ready to let our minds cease activity and come to a point of absolute quiet. In the soft movement of our breath, and the peacefulness of our minds, we find the hand of God massaging our souls into something new. We make a commitment to a small step of action and feel ready to go forward with gratitude for the time we have spent with God.

Ignatian Prayer is based on the Ignatian Exercises developed by Ignatius of Loyola in the early 1500s to help retreatants identify God's will and follow through on it in their daily lives. Ignatian meditation uses the mind and the senses to better understand the biblical story and to enter more fully into it in order to change behavior. Through the process of prayer we begin to see our strengths and weaknesses, where our habits have become our prisons, and what we can do to better enflesh the life of Jesus in our own lives.

The meditation begins with a brief time of centering to acknowledge that we are in the presence of God. After we make an intention for the prayer time, we slowly work through the chosen scripture passage by mentally placing ourselves at the scene. We try to imagine all the details of the space/place as a preparation for applying all of our senses imaginatively to the scene. If a Gospel passage is selected, the connection between us and the life of Jesus is strengthened. As we enter the story, we encounter Christ and are led to ask ourselves and Jesus what needs to be attended to in our lives, what needs further reflection, what waits to open us to a new way of being. In this intimate encounter we find a desire to become more than we were before, to give ourselves more fully to the Creator and lover of our souls.

When we have imagined the scene, applied our senses to it, met Jesus in it, and identified ways in which we can carry it into our lives, we find ourselves in a discourse or conversation with Jesus that deepens intimacy and leads to personal growth and change. The meditation comes to a close with a prayer such as the Lord's Prayer. At any point in the reflection or at the end of the conversation, we may find our souls becoming still and our hearts longing only to sit with Jesus in silence and contemplation. The very work that engages the mind becomes the food for contemplative prayer.

If you find your soul longing more for sitting meditation than thinking meditation, you may find patterns of discursive meditation unsettling at first. After a few days, however, the hunger for reflection creates a longing to dig even more deeply into the stories that have the potential to re-work the outlines of your soul. On the other hand, if you are immediately drawn to this type of meditation because you appreciate the thoughtful, reflective, and logical style of it, you will be surprised when that very thinking and reflecting unexpectedly leads to simply being still and quiet.

4 ▪ Mindfulness

. . . What all this is about, remember, is trying to feel fully alive, to keep ourselves and the earth alive. And, as Thoreau was to say in so many ways, that means living fully in the present. For most of us, our attention is constantly diverted. We're rarely aware of what we are doing.

Take food. Food is probably one of the best symbols of our American way of life. Food is meant to nourish us, but it is also meant to be enjoyed. And the only way you can enjoy it is to pay attention to your eating. But we never do that. Our contribution to world cuisine is fast food. What does it mean to have drive-through windows to get our food? We have invented food that can be eaten with one hand while we're doing something else. It's pathological. We're not tasting the food; we're not getting any real pleasure or even nourishment out of it. And with all the chemicals and petroleum involved in our food production, our way of eating is destroying the planet as well. In other words, we're trashing the planet for something we are not even enjoying.

So one way of being mindful is paying attention to and savoring what you eat.

When you eat, focus on enjoying eating.

In living mindfully, we pay attention to whatever we're doing and "suck out all the marrow," as Thoreau said. We become deeply absorbed in what we are doing, appreciating the people we are with, being conscious of the wind on our face. It means paying attention to what you are doing, and not doing ten things at once. Taking the time to notice, slowing down, sitting peacefully, and just being.

Time Anxiety

Being mindful is hard for us because we are always anxious about time. Just as we never feel we have enough money, we never have enough time. In fact, maybe it's because we feel we don't have enough money that we feel that we don't have enough time. Since we measure everything in terms of money, that sense of scarcity pervades our whole life. Learning that we have enough—money, time, love—may be our most important lesson.

Even when we eliminate the apparent obstacles of working and consuming too much, we still have trouble relaxing and enjoying the present moment. So the problem is not just the scarcity of time, it's our attitude toward time. That little voice always creeps in, You'd better hurry, you've got a lot to do, you're not getting enough done, time is running out. What does this mean in terms of feeling alive? Surely, if things keep on this way, when we come to die, we will discover that we have not lived.

We live in constant anticipation of the future, regret and guilt over the past: we can hardly wait for the weekend, for summer vacation, for the kids to be grown up, until retirement. We might as well say, "I can hardly wait until I die."

In the past I read books that told how to get more done during the day, how to find that extra hour so you could study French or learn photography. I would try to do as many things as I could at one time. Now I focus on doing less and slowing down. I try to stop rushing, to practice mindfulness, to practice meditation. I keep working at it, but still I have that nagging feeling—hurry, hurry.

We get upset at everything that gets in our way. We yell at other drivers, using language that shocks us. We switch checkout lanes in the grocery stores, we click through TV shows, we hurry our kids.

Once, in a frantic effort to get ready for a birthday party for my kids, I tried to blow up balloons while I was driving.

Is it the universe's revenge? We, who have ruined the earth's resources, have had our only true resource, time, ruined for us. We are a caricature of a whirling dervish. We have made a mockery of so many of the world's spiritual traditions—all of which warn against excessive greed—that we've been set spinning, unable to stop and enjoy life.

I try not to rush and to move slowly as I clean the kitchen. But my husband, who doesn't think about these issues as much as I do, who is still in a traditional job, undergoes a personality change every Monday morning—starting to frown, starting to be impatient, intent on beating the clock. As Thoreau said, "As if we could kill time without injuring eternity." And we are killing time. That used to mean just sitting around; but now, in our frenzied activity, we really are killing time. So much of our time is spent in ways that kill our spirit, our capacity to enjoy the moment, to experience the depth of the moment. Americans, who are so egocentric, think we have built the best possible civilization, but we have no time to enjoy it.

And why? Because time has become money. What a joke. We value money above all. We measure our most precious commodity, time, in terms of money, and find that we can't enjoy time at all. A Faustian bargain. You want to have all the money in the world? Okay, you can have money, but no time to enjoy life.

Sometimes I will go into my husband's study as he sits there writing on his computer and say to him, "Well, this is it! This is your life! It's probably not going to get any better!" How else can I remind him, and myself, to take time seriously, to not let it slip away.

To live mindfully, to appreciate your time, you have to move slowly.

There's nothing more difficult for Americans, and we have gotten worse in the last twenty years. Court reporters find that we talk faster. We walk faster, our movies are faster. MTV is the perfect example. Just as you start to focus on an image, the camera moves on.

What is this addiction to stimulation? Sometimes I feel addicted to my own adrenaline. If I'm not rushing, feeling pressured, I feel like I'm missing something. Is this the only way we can feel alive now—by rushing? Are we mistaking the rush of caffeine for a feeling of vitality? Does rushing make us feel like we are doing something important, that we are important people? Are we all engaged in such meaningless work that we can only feel important if we feel pressured? Do we have to convince ourselves and others of the importance of our work to justify our existence?

Here is where mindfulness comes in. You must pay attention to your speed and consciously slow down. Maybe make that your mantra—slow down—saying it very slowly . . . of course, in our rushing, we have no time to talk with people, so we get lonelier and lonelier.

In rushing, we have no time for reflection, no time to notice what is going on around us. We can't reflect on warning signals that come to us—warning signals such as early signs that something is wrong with our health. Signs that you are starting to drive too fast. For instance, whenever I have a near miss in my car, I always say to myself, "Ahh, a message from the universe," and I slow down and become more careful in my driving.

Once I walked in on a man in the process of robbing my house. On my walk up to the door I had noticed several little things I later realized should have told me what was happening. But I ignored them. I escaped unharmed, but once again I thought to myself, "You ignored the signs. You didn't pay attention."

When we rush, we are much more likely to consume because we are ignoring the little voice asking us if we really need this new thing. Impulse buying is what corporations depend on.

I think that little voice is always there speaking to us, telling us the right thing to do, but we ignore it because we are rushing and have no time to listen.

This is what I would like to feel more than anything. Gratitude. How else can you really enjoy your life? To feel gratitude is to look at everything in your life and appreciate it, be aware of it, pay attention to it. Our lifestyle, of course, engenders discontent and resentment. Because more is always better, you can never be satisfied with what you have. Because commercials are constantly showing us ecstatically happy people with lots of stuff, we always feel that we're just not quite making it. Then, when we see how much money rich people have, we feel envious. All of these feelings make you discontent with your life, causing you to fail to be grateful for what you do have.

5 ■ Spaciousness

Every risk we take for love, each step we take toward greater consecration, leads us deeper into the spaciousness of love. In biblical Hebrew, the letters *yodh* and *shin* combine to form a root that connotes "space and the freedom and security which is gained by the removal of constriction." From this YS root come words like *yesha* and *yeshuah*, referring to salvation. When you think about it, it makes sense that space would be intimately associated with salvation. Space is freedom: freedom from confinement, from preoccupation, from oppression, from drivenness, and from all the other interior and exterior forces that bind and restrict our spirits. We need space in the first place simply to recognize how compelled and bound we are. Then we need space to allow the compulsions to ease and the bonds to loosen. In the Hebrew sense, our passion needs elbow room. To the extent that space is permitted by grace and our own willingness, we discover expanding emptiness in which consecration can happen, room for love to make its home in us.

Spaciousness comes to us in three primary ways. First, it appears as spaciousness of *form*: physical, geographic spaces like the wide openness of fields, water, and sky and the welcoming simplicity of uncluttered rooms. Second, it comes as spaciousness of *time*: pauses in activity when we are freed from tasks, agendas, and other demands. Third, we encounter spaciousness of *soul*. This is inner emptiness, the room inside our hearts, the unfulfilled quality of our consciousness. Depending upon how we meet this soul-space, we may experience it as open possibility or void nothingness, as creative potential or dulling boredom, as quiet, peaceful serenity or as restless yearning for fulfillment.

People in our modern developed world are ambivalent about all three kinds of spaciousness. On the one hand, we long for space; in the midst of overactive lives we yearn for peace, stillness, and freedom. We look forward to vacations, and we yearn for our minds to be free of preoccupation. On the other hand, we are liable to become very uncomfortable when such spaces do open up. We do not seem to know what to do with them. We fill up our vacations with activities and compulsions; we fill up our minds with worries and obsessions. We know we need rest, but we can no longer see the value of rest as an end in itself; it is only worthwhile if it helps us recharge our batteries so we can be even more efficient in the next period of productivity.

The ancients knew the value of spaciousness for its own sake. The Hebrews ritualized the Sabbath in keeping with God's rest on the seventh day of creation. God did not take that day of rest simply to recoup energy to begin creating another universe during the next workweek. Resting was valuable in its own right. Spaciousness was holy.

The fourth commandment for Jews and Christians is to remember the Sabbath and keep it holy. Many other religions and denominations continue to provide for such times of space and rest, but the meaning has often been twisted. Sabbath was meant to be a day of spaciousness in form, time, and soul. It was to be an uncluttered day, a day not filled up, a day of rest and appreciation, a day of freedom just to be. Now, religious Sabbath is apt to feel like restriction rather than freedom, confinement rather than space. Instead of freedom from having to work, Sabbath came to mean not being *allowed* to work.

We have clearly lost something when we are no longer free just to be, when we must always be active, doing some things and refraining from doing others. Something is missing when we have to force our pauses, carve out our spaces, and then feel we have to justify them. As a result, recreation often means engaging in more pleasurable work, not freedom from having to work at all. Something is amiss when wasting time is something we feel ashamed of, when we must ask a quiet person, "What's wrong?" It is as if a piece of the heart has been cut out; our capacity to be easeful with inactivity has been thrown away and forgotten without our even realizing it.

Think about yourself. How are you when there is nothing to do? When you have a moment of freedom, what do you do with it? Try to take such a moment now: no agenda, nothing to accomplish, just be. Stay with it as long as you can. What happens? Does it feel freeing or confining, peaceful or anxious? Was it different when you were a child? Did it come more easily and feel more comfortable then? If so, what do you think accounts for the change?

Most of us, most of the time, just fill our spaces up or dull our awareness of them. We grab a book, run to the television, work on a project, socialize, have a drink. We somehow must realign our attitudes toward spaciousness. We must begin to see it as presence rather than absence, friend instead of enemy. This is the most important practical challenge we face in being consciously in love. It will not be easy, because we have come to associate space with fear, emptiness with negativity, lack of fulfillment with dysfunction. The seventeenth-century philosopher Benedict de Spinoza said that nature abhors a vacuum. Modern science has shown he was wrong. There is far more space than stuff in the universe. The atoms that make up all matter, including our own bodies, consist of vast distances of space between tiny subatomic particles. No matter how solid we may feel, we are much more space than substance. If any nature abhors a vacuum, it is human nature—and that only because our nature has been so adulterated by conditioning.

Give yourself a little space. Take a moment and just sit, just be. Waste some time. See and hear what there is around you, and notice what happens within you. Do not expect any particular experience, and do not contrive anything. How does it go?

Space and Repression

It is an addiction of the first order that we feel we must always be filling up our spaces. It goes along with our addictions to work, to productivity, to efficiency. Sometimes, though, we do not like spaciousness because of what appears to us within it. Ever since Sigmund Freud's work, psychology has understood that human beings try to keep unpleasant things out of awareness. The psychoanalysts called it repression or suppression; a more modern term is selective inattention.

At any given moment, we all have a number of worries, fears, guilt feelings, bad memories, and things we are procrastinating about that we are simply putting out of our minds. The difficulty with space, especially interior spaciousness of soul, is that it allows such repressed and suppressed annoyances back into awareness.

When I pause for a moment and let my mind settle down, what comes in? The things I have put off, the worries I have been avoiding, the bad feelings I have stifled. Space is like sunlight and fresh air toward which the buried uglies of our souls crawl in search of healing. It is a very healthy thing. Space is not only potentially restful but also therapeutic. But like many therapeutic processes, it can be painful. And in matters of healing consciousness, as in love, there can be no anesthesia.

It is also possible to create fake space, in which we force our minds into stillness and keep everything repressed. In fact, it is this fake space that most people associate with meditation and concentration—a forceful, effortful attempt to keep the mind silent, focused, and without "distraction." But this is not space at all. It is instead a kind of trance, a deadening of sensitivity, a stifling and restriction of awareness. It is anesthetized; there is no openness in it, no willingness, no participation. True space is encountered only with the willingness and courage to experience things just as they are.

When people tell me they have trouble taking time for prayer or meditation, I often ask them what unpleasant things they might be wanting to avoid. I often ask myself the same question. My answer right now is ironic; the thing I most want to escape from is my longing for love. It hurts too much, more than anything psychological I have ever experienced. There are many times I would escape it or anesthetize it if I could, but it will not go away. Or perhaps *I* cannot go away.

It is a blessing when love is so relentless, because the more we repress, suppress, procrastinate, or anesthetize, the more resistant we will be toward space. Conversely, the more true space we give ourselves, the less we will repress. And to the extent that we consecrate our spaciousness, intend it for love, point it toward love's source, space will be merciful. The unpleasantness of space will never be more than we can bear. Our increasing availability to the truth happens gradually, gently, with grace. It happens in keeping with our own unique personalities; we are given what we need as we need it. Space becomes brutal only if we try to force it, make it a project, or demand that it meet our expectations.

At the turn of the fifteenth century, Julian of Norwich wrote, "I learned to be afraid of my instability. For I do not know in what way I shall fall. I would have liked to have known that—with due fear, of course. But I got no answer." She faced her fear and was able to continue: "Both when we fall and when we get up again we are kept in the same precious love. The love in which God made us never had beginning. In it we have our beginning."[1]

Spaciousness is always a beginning, a possibility, a potential, a capacity for birth. Space exists not in order to be filled but to create. In space, to the extent we can bear the truth of the way things are, we find the ever-beginning presence of love. Take the time, then; make the space. Seek it wherever you can find it, do it however you can. The manner does not matter, and the experience you have there is of secondary importance. Seek the truth, not what is comfortable. Seek the real, not the easy.

Perhaps you already have an intentional rhythm of prayer, meditation, or reflection. If so, the form may not need to change at all. Just review what you do and what seems to happen. Does your practice allow some real space, or has it become completely filled with spiritual activity? Is it a time of immediate presence for you, in which you can just be? Or has it become a routine in which you find more dullness than wakefulness, more focused attention than openness to what is?

The first step is to look for spaces that occur naturally in your life. We all have them, and they can tell us something about what is uniquely right for us. Perhaps you find little natural spaces after

---

1. From chaps. 79, 82, and 86 of the long version of her "Shewings" (from Sloane Manuscript 2499), in Julian of Norwich, *Revelations of Divine Love*, trans. Clifton Wolters (New York: Penguin, 1982), 203, 208, 212.

you have completed some work, times that you stretch and look around and just be for a moment. Could times like that be expanded? Could you savor them a little longer? Or maybe you sometimes indulge in a long, hot bath, or find yourself in stillness just before you go to sleep or wake up. Possibly you find space in nature or gardening, in music or exercise. Take a while to go over a typical day in your mind—where are the most likely moments of spaciousness? Are there some such moments that you usually immediately fill by watching television, reading, drinking, or some other activity that dulls you even though you call it recreation? Might you be able to just be present a while longer in some of those moments before you move to fill or dull yourself? Might some of them be expanded and made more intentional without causing them to feel too contrived or artificial?

In addition, you should probably at least try to set aside some regular time each day, in the morning or evening or both, that is simply and solely dedicated to just being. In the beginning, these times may be only a few minutes long. A friend of mine began each morning with only the time it took her coffee to percolate. I think there is little value in staying there longer than you can remain fresh and present. When busy-ness and dullness take over, it is probably best to move on and come back again later. On the other hand, don't run away when the first repressed unpleasantness surfaces. Try to let it be; stay a little longer with what is.

A set-aside time in the morning, however brief, can establish a kind of attitudinal posture (*disposition* is the classical word) for beginning the day. It is a time when you can consecrate the day and yourself for the day, offering your prayer for greater presence in love. Likewise, evening times can include a little reflection on the day. Where were the moments of space? What times seemed to contain real presence? What glimpses of being in love were you given? What enterprises or situations kidnapped you and held you hostage to functioning or fear? And where is the spaciousness right now, in this moment at the end of the day? What do you seek there? What is the deepest desire with which you might drift into sleep?

Finally, keep an eye open for longer spaces. Consider extended spiritual retreats, quiet days, or contemplative prayer or meditation groups where you can spend some dedicated and less distracted time just simply being. Bear in mind that I am not speaking of the talk- and activity-filled conferences that are sometimes called retreats or spiritual groups, but of periods in which people truly seek stillness and deepening alone or together. Experiment with whether you find space more easily alone or with other people. Look to your own Sabbath—is it possible to claim some time like that for yourself, when just being is truly an end in itself? What sort of support might you need from other people to help you pursue this?

I have proposed that you seek three kinds of spaces in your life: little moments in the midst of work and play, regular set-aside times each day, and periodic longer times of authentic retreat. In all these, and in the rest of your time as well, I hope you will seek the spaciousness of the immediate moment: the spaciousness of *presence*. In this one single moment, here and now, all three kinds of spaciousness come together: form because it is here, time because it is now, and soul because aliveness is birthed in immediacy.

You will, as I do, find yourself resisting the spaciousness of presence. Sometimes you will know that you simply do not want to face into it; it may seem too painful, or it may require too much letting-go of other investments. That is all right. Do not try to force it. If you fight for presence simply because you think you *should*, you will only stifle yourself. True presence never comes through coercion.

But there will be other times, increasingly frequent, when you know that in spite of your resistance you really do desire presence; you want it deeply regardless of the pain it holds or the relinquishment you must endure.

The emptiness of the spaciousness of the present moment is sufficient. It contains everything that is needed for lovingly beginning the next moment; it seeks only our own willing, responsive presence, just here, just now. And we can bear whatever experience we have in the spaciousness of this present moment. If we project it into the future it may seem impossible, but just here, just now, it is not too much. There are no exceptions—not in physical pain, not in psychiatric disorder or emotional agony, not in relational strife, not in war, not in oppression, not in loss, not in spiritual aching, not in dying. Love is too much with us for there to be any exceptions.

6 ■ Silence

We've all had them. Those weeks when the world seems too full of suffering, too full of hatred, too full of complications and questions that appear to have no answers. Recently I had one of those weeks, and I am still struggling today, wishing my spirit had more lightness, wishing I could feel as great as the day looks. It is a clear and sunny spring day, and the buds of spring are beginning to burst.

In Illinois, a young, promising graduate student opened fire on fellow students, killing six and traumatizing an entire community. In New York City, a therapist was murdered with a meat cleaver in her private practice office by a man who was unhappy with treatment he had received some years ago. She wasn't even the one who treated him, not that it really matters. A colleague confides in me that more and more of the young adult/college-age population he treats have clinical psychosis, a loss of contact with reality. A friend's brother completes suicide. A neighbor's child is diagnosed with a malignant tumor.

What is happening? Certainly, I do not claim to have any hold on the complexities of the world. But I do relate to a sermon I read recently. Entitled "The Walrus of the Living God," it was preached on January 8, 2008, by Maggie Ross, an Anglican solitary and author residing in the United Kingdom. In this sermon, Ms. Ross suggests that not only is the ecology of our planet Earth out of balance, but the ecology of our souls is in severe disarray as well. She states plainly and simply that our souls require silence. Our souls were designed to be in silence and are finely tuned when they experience their core silence.

Now that may give us a clue about what is wrong. At least it's a sliver of an answer to a problem that feels bottomless, like a black hole. Silence. I am not saying that silence is a cure for mental illness, although I can imagine that a calmer life might help those suffering with such illnesses. Some silence might help us make better choices, might slow down the impulsivity of our choices. Some silence, some entering into the Heart of our heart, could reestablish the balance between what is real and personal and what is being projected onto others.

If you are an urban or suburban dweller, when was the last time you had real silence? A client told me recently that her home lost power for several hours. The "silence," she reported, was almost overpowering. The refrigerator wasn't humming, the HVAC wasn't cranking up, the TV wasn't making background noise, the home phone wasn't ringing, the fluorescent light in her kitchen was quiet. Total silence. *Weird at first*, she thought, and then a bit uncomfortable. Even outside the house, where only the sounds of nature were present, was silent. But as the hours wore on, she settled in, lit some candles, and let herself feel the gift of a few silent hours. "Balm for my soul," she said.

If you are younger than forty, when was the last time you experienced silence? Most of the people who would fit into this category know about being plugged in. The cell phone is always on, and "texting" is a 24/7 activity. Many high school and college students sleep with their phones next to them in bed and receive texts and phone messages throughout the night. Even sleep isn't silent any more. And waking? In addition to cell phones, there are iPods, iPads, computers, radios, televisions, video games, PDAs, busy malls, and the like to keep us eternally plugged in. Where is the room for silence?

If we are to experience God's reality, I believe we must *make* room for it. If our brains are constantly bombarded with noise, the ecology of our souls will begin to disintegrate. We are designed to know ourselves and to know God through the silence of the soul. Dare I say that in our silence we have the opportunity to remember who God is and remember who we are?

How do we fight the cultural norm of noisiness? We could turn off the TV, radio, iPod, and computer, maybe for just a thirty-minute period. Even eating dinner without any accompanying noise could be a beginning. We could try sitting in silence for ten minutes a day, doing nothing but paying attention to our breath. Better yet, visiting a garden, park, or green space to help us stay attuned to the natural world might silence our inner chatter and reestablish in us a sense of the order of creation. Would our schools be willing to offer a period of silence, maybe just five minutes at a time? Could those of us in churches ask for longer periods of silence? How could we teach our youth the value of silence? Of contemplation? Of listening?

We must be willing to give up the familiar noise and risk what we might encounter when we become silent. My own experience with silence is that it will bring questions and it will bring answers. It will bring suffering and it will bring hope. It will challenge me and it will soothe me. Like anything that is real, it will be paradoxical. When we touch the heart of God through practiced silence, nothing will remain the same. That is the fear and that is the hope. When Augustine said, "Without God, we cannot; without us, God will not," I think he knew the critical importance of communing with God through silence. Perhaps it is one way to start making real changes.

7 ■ Doing Nothing

The final chapter of *The House at Pooh Corner* is achingly sad. This is the chapter where Christopher Robin is about to go away to school. After a farewell gathering he takes Pooh to an enchanted place on the other side of the forest and tries to explain to him the strange mysteries of growing up. But these are things he doesn't quite understand himself, so he struggles to find the words that will convey the rapid changes that lie ahead of him and the enormity of the things he must leave behind.

As they walk along they chat about this and that, and Christopher Robin asks Pooh what he likes doing best in all the world. Pooh begins to say that eating honey is the best thing, but then he reflects that there is "a moment just before you began to eat it which was better than when you were, but he didn't know what it was called." This seems to me to be a profound reflection borne of a real appreciation of the glorious giftedness of life. Some things are so beautiful, so satisfying, so desirable that the anticipation of receiving them is almost better than the receiving itself. Though the wonder of the receiving overwhelms you, there is something uniquely special about dwelling in the moment of anticipation.

There are certain pieces of piano music that give me this feeling. I am, of course, thinking of particular pieces of music—one of Chopin's nocturnes or Mendelssohn's *Songs without Words*. I am thinking of these pieces because they were played by my mother and seem to have accompanied me throughout my life. But it is not just the music I am thinking of, nor the memories the music evokes, but the sense of wonder that music is made up of the notes themselves and also the silence between the notes. And all these are both given in the writing down of the music and endlessly re-created in the different interpretations of each individual performance. If it is a piece you know well, there is, sometimes, in a new interpretation, a moment of tremulous expectation when the pianist pauses for a fraction of a second that can seem like an eternity, and the anticipation of what is to come, that single longed-for note, enhances and heightens the beauty when at last it is played.

Can the whole of my life be such a moment of ecstatic anticipation, waiting to hear the completion of the music I already know: the music of creation that made me, that plays in the universe around me, that beckons from the God who composed me?

Most of the time the answer must be no, I am simply too bound up with my own ambitions and trivialities, too self-centered and self-seeking to enter into the possibilities that are right in front of me. But sometimes it is different. That is all that this book has been about—the sustaining glimpses of these differences, and the hope that they might multiply, changing my life and changing the world. Or, to put it another way, when you start to live with the appreciation that everything you experience in this life comes from God, then you can live each moment as an anticipation of the delight that awaits you when you see God face to face.

But Pooh has an even deeper wisdom to impart. There are some things even better than the anticipated delight of eating honey. It was being with the people he loves. He eventually concludes that the very best thing in all the world is for "Me and Piglet going to see You [Christopher Robin], and You saying 'What about a little something?' and Me saying, 'Well, I shouldn't mind a little something, should you, Piglet,' and it being a hummy sort of day outside, and birds singing."

Here Pooh adds to his first observation that true happiness can be found as much in the anticipation of delight as in the delight itself, by saying that this delight can only truly be enjoyed when it is in the company of others.

I can't read this passage without thinking of the Christian Eucharist: the service of Holy Communion, which is at the heart of Christian worship. Here bread and wine are broken and shared in remembrance of the meal Jesus shared with his friends on the night before he died. The meal, however, signifies more than fellowship. It is enacted parable, indicating the meaning of his death on the cross. Like the bread that is broken and the wine poured out, Jesus' body will be broken on the cross and his blood shed. These will be the sufferings he faces before his risen life can be shared.

In the Christian Eucharist we receive the life of Christ. His life is shared with us. The breaking of the bread and the pouring of the wine remind us of his actions and draw us into the meaning of the cross. Christians believe that God uses the bread and wine to feed those who come to him in faith. The invitation to share the bread and wine, and the communion itself, anticipates that eternal moment of God's eternity when we will dwell in the presence of God and gather at the heavenly banquet. In other words it is a meal held in the company of friends, in which we receive the life of heaven that the meal anticipates. Indeed, the word "company," and the word "companion" that is derived from it, come from the French meaning, literally, "one with whom we break bread."

It is then Christopher Robin's turn to answer his own question. And his answer leads us back to the central message of this book and to the great Sabbath rest that the Jewish and Christian faiths describe as the climax of God's creation. "What I like *doing* best," says Christopher Robin, "is Nothing."

"How do you do Nothing?" asks Pooh, after he had wondered for a long time. "Well, it's when people call out at you just as you're going off to do it, 'What are you going to do, Christopher Robin?' and you say 'Oh nothing,' and then you go and do it. It means just going along, listening to all the things you can't hear, and not bothering."

Listening to the things you can't hear. Seeing the things you can't see. Loving the things you can't feel. Here we are very close to the topsy-turvy absurdity of Christian faith. For at its heart, the Christian faith has a conviction that the deepest reality abides in those things that cannot be seen or heard. Faith itself, says the New Testament, "is the assurance of things hoped for, the conviction of things not seen" (Hebrews 11.1).

The world around us is real, it is beautiful and God can be found in it. But it will pass away. This is what is known about all created things. They live and they die. The earth makes its constant orbit round the sun and from it receives the energy needed for life. But even the sun will burn itself out, and this universe, which is inexorably expanding, will, one day, when time itself ceases to be, contract upon itself and be no more. This living and dying is all around us. You see it in the pattern of the seasons, in all the tiny deaths that make up human life, and in the vast, aching tragedies of individual lives lost or broken. You cannot escape it. It is with you every day and it waits for you at the day that will be your last.

But there is another, deeper reality. Not a reality that is separate from what you see and feel, but behind it and between it; a reality that has no beginning or end, that is uncreated, and upon which everything else rests. It is quite possible to go through all of life not noticing this reality. It is quite possible to doubt it and disbelieve it. There is plenty of evidence to suppose that such a claim is wistful madness. Earthquakes, cancer, human hatred, prejudice, all do more than enough to chip away at any hope that the universe may be lovable. And yet this hope persists. It lives cheek by jowl with misery and danger, and despite the tremendous capacity of human freedom to create and destroy, human beings go on hoping.

People go on hoping because the things that are unseen, the things that are felt and believed, seem somehow to be more certain. Through them we glimpse the possibility of God, and we dare to hope that beyond the last breath of the last moment of this life, there is something else. This something else is called the eternal presence of God. It is a presence that has created and sustains the universe. It is a presence that awaits us at the end. When we try to capture it, it eludes us. This is not a God who can be pinned down, or clung to, or constrained by definitions and dogmas. Many good people, in trying to define and capture the presence of God, have ended up destroying it. The rules and regulations of religion have often suffocated the life of the Spirit. Nevertheless, the great religions of the world teach us to reach beyond ourselves. Their definitions and dogmas are not pigeonholes but growbags; well-fertilized soil in which faith and hope can grow. And the Christian way—this religion that is not a religion—this strange, participative drama in which the invisible God becomes flesh, offers an invitation to a different sort of living in which every moment is a foretaste of glory and an opportunity to discern and celebrate the presence of God.

In the Creation story at the beginning of the Bible we are told that God labored for six days in the great work of creation but on the seventh day, seeing the goodness and harmony of all that had been made, rested. This seventh day is the day God has hallowed. It is a day of rest and celebration that is a gift in creation. It is also the fourth of the Ten Commandments: Remember the Sabbath day and keep it holy.

For us, in the busy Western world, any sense of a special day of rest and re-creation has long since disappeared. Sunday is just like any other day. The boundaries between the different days of the week, the seasons of the year, and even, nowadays, between night and day, have been eroded. This brings a terrible loss. People are deprived of the rhythms and patterns that shape life. And with this, the pressure to be busy and productive increases. There is less time for family, less time for leisure, less time for the re-creation, which is the purpose of leisure.

Christians and non-Christians alike may crave for a return to a more ordered rhythm to the week, but it seems unlikely that this will come about in the near future. Therefore, rather than fighting a rear-guard action to keep Sunday special, it might be better to consider how you can build some Sabbath time into the schedules and rhythms of the life you have. These are the disciplines of slowing down and shutting up that were explored in the last chapter. They are a recovery of Sabbath, the creation of a place of rest where joy and contentment can flourish.

So let's spend more time listening to the things we can't hear and therefore coming closer to the things we cannot see. This will not only prepare us for heaven, it will enable us to live the life of heaven, the true Sabbath, here on earth.

In doing nothing; in taking rest and play seriously; in unmasking the illusion that meaning and value can only be found in busyness and so-called productivity; in learning to cherish the present moment, we discover that God can best be found in the silences between the notes; in what is written between the lines. Not through our effort, or hard work, or even our goodness, but in those moments of forgetfulness, of sleeping and dreaming, when we are suddenly caught unawares by the wild and mysterious beauty of the world. This is the Sabbath rest that the Christian Scriptures promise: a place of homecoming and a place of creativity.

So switch off the TV; put this book down; shut your eyes; breathe deeply; dream; do nothing but listen to the things you can't hear. Nurture your inner slob. You might even find you begin to pray—not by saying a lot of stuff to God, but by enjoying the intimacy of God's presence and the fragile beauty of each passing moment.

To put it another way: don't just do something, sit there!

TURN: Pause, listen, and choose to follow Jesus

THE WAY OF LOVE

As Jesus was walking along, he saw Levi son of Alphaeus sitting at the tax booth, and he said to him, "Follow me." And he got up and followed him. – Mark 2:14

"Do you turn to Jesus Christ . . . ?" – Book of Common Prayer, 302

Like the disciples, we are called by Jesus to follow the Way of Love. With God's help, we can turn from the powers of sin, hatred, fear, injustice, and oppression toward the way of truth, love, hope, justice, and freedom. In turning, we reorient our lives to Jesus Christ, falling in love again, again, and again.

For Reflection and Discernment

- What practices help you to turn again and again to Jesus and the Way of Love?
- How will (or do) you incorporate these practices into your rhythm of life?
- Who will be your companion as you turn toward Jesus?

LEARN: Reflect on Scripture each day, especially on Jesus's life and teachings.

"Those who love me will keep my word, and my Father will love them, and we will come to them and make our home with them." – John 14:23

Grant us so to hear [the Holy Scriptures], read, mark, learn, and inwardly digest them. – Book of Common Prayer, 236

By reading and reflecting on Scripture, especially the life and teachings of Jesus, we draw near to God, and God's word dwells in us. When we open our minds and hearts to Scripture, we learn to see God's story and God's activity in everyday life.

For Reflection and Discernment

- What ways of reflecting on Scripture are most life-giving for you?
- When will you set aside time to read and reflect on Scripture in your day?
- With whom will you share in the commitment to read and reflect on Scripture?

PRAY: Dwell intentionally with God daily

He was praying in a certain place, and after he had finished,
one of his disciples said to him, "Lord, teach us to pray,
as John taught his disciples." – Luke 11:1

"Lord, hear our prayer." – Book of Common Prayer

Jesus teaches us to come before God with humble hearts, boldly offering our
thanksgivings and concerns to God or simply listening for God's voice in our
lives and in the world. Whether in thought, word, or deed, individually or
corporately, when we pray we invite and dwell in God's loving presence.

For Reflection and Discernment

- What intentional prayer practices center you in God's presence, so
  you can hear, speak, or simply dwell with God?
- How will (or do) you incorporate intentional prayer into your daily life?
- With whom will you share in the commitment to pray?

WORSHIP: Gather in community weekly to thank, praise, and dwell with God

When he was at the table with them, he took bread, blessed and broke it,
and gave it to them. Then their eyes were opened, and they recognized him.
– Luke 24:30-31

Celebrant: Lift up your hearts. People: We lift them to the Lord.
– Book of Common Prayer, 361

When we worship, we gather with others before God. We hear the Good
News of Jesus, give thanks, confess, and offer the brokenness of the world to
God. As we break bread, our eyes are opened to the presence of Christ. By the
power of the Holy Spirit, we are made one body, the body of Christ sent forth
to live the Way of Love.

For Discernment and Reflection

- What communal worship practices move you to encounter God and
  knit you into the body of Christ?
- How will (or do) you commit to regularly worship?
- With whom will you share the commitment to worship this week?

BLESS: Share faith and unselfishly give and serve

"Freely you have received; freely give." – Matthew 10:8

Celebrant: Will you proclaim by word and example the Good News of God in Christ?
People: We will, with God's help. – Book of Common Prayer, 305

Jesus called his disciples to give, forgive, teach, and heal in his name. We are empowered by the Spirit to bless everyone we meet, practicing generosity and compassion and proclaiming the Good News of God in Christ with hopeful words and selfless actions. We can share our stories of blessing and invite others to the Way of Love.

For Discernment and Reflection

- What are the ways the Spirit is calling you to bless others?
- How will (or does) blessing others through sharing your resources, faith, and story become part of your daily life?
- Who will join you in committing to the practice of blessing others

GO: Cross boundaries, listen deeply, and live like Jesus

Jesus said to them, "Peace be with you. As the Father has sent me,
so I send you." – John 20:21

Send them into the world in witness to your love.
– Book of Common Prayer, 306

As Jesus went to the highways and byways, he sends us beyond our circles and comfort to witness to the love, justice, and truth of God with our lips and with our lives. We go to listen with humility and to join God in healing a hurting world. We go to become Beloved Community, a people reconciled in love with God and one another.

For Discernment and Reflection

- To what new places or communities is the Spirit sending you to witness to the love, justice, and truth of God?
- How will you build into your life a commitment to cross boundaries, listen carefully, and take part in healing and reconciling what is broken in this world?
- With whom will you share in the commitment to go forth as a reconciler and healer?

REST: Receive the gift of God's grace, peace, and restoration

*Peace I leave with you; my peace I give you. I do not give to you
as the world gives. Do not let your hearts be troubled
and do not be afraid. – John 14:27*

*Blessed are you, O Lord . . . giving rest to the weary,
renewing the strength of those who are spent.
– Book of Common Prayer, 113*

From the beginning of creation, god has established the sacred pattern of
going and returning, labor and rest. Especially today, God invites us to dedi-
cate time for restoration and wholeness—within our bodies, minds, and souls,
and within our communities and institutions. By resting, we place our trust in
God; the primary actor who brings all things to their fullness.

For Discernment and Reflection

- What practices restore your body, mind and soul?
- How will you observe rest and renewal on a regular basis?
- With whom will you commit to create and maintain a regular
  practice of rest?